Insider Secrets About How To Quickly and Easily Pay Off Your Debts

Insider Secrets About How To Quickly and Easily Pay Off Your Debts

AND DIRTY LITTLE SECRETS
YOUR BANKER NEVER
WANTS YOU TO KNOW

● ● ●

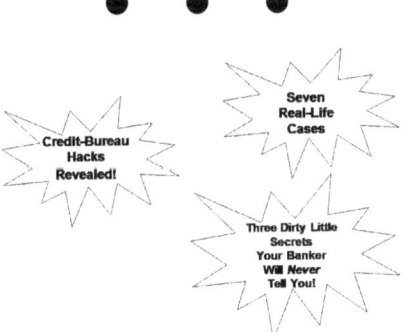

Charles H Bristoll

© 2018 Charles H Bristoll
All rights reserved.

ISBN-13: 9781545461228
ISBN-10: 1545461228

Contents

Introduction vii

Chapter 1 Why Did My Bank Decline Me? 1
Case Study 1: Robert and Sarah's
Credit Crunch 6
Chapter 2 How Much Money Can I Get? 9
Case Study 2: Peter's Investment
Emergency 13
Chapter 3 What Will My Payment Be? 15
Case Study 3: Katherine and David's
Tears of Joy 22
Chapter 4 I'm Self-Employed. Is That Okay? 25
Case Study 4: Dimitri's Parents 29
Chapter 5 Who Is the Lender? 32
Case Study 5: Sean the Contractor 36
Chapter 6 How Does the Appraisal Work? 39
Case Study 6: Tim's Start-up 47
Chapter 7 What If I Have Bad Credit? 50
Case Study 7: Jay's Partner Buyout 59

Chapter 8	What Are the Costs Involved?	62
	Case Study 8: Victor's Illness Kills His Credit	70
Chapter 9	Why Is There a Lawyer Involved?	73
Chapter 10	The Debt Miracle	76

Introduction

• • •

My name is Charles Bristoll. Early in my career, while working for a bank, I watched helplessly as one of the bank's customers, a hardworking man with three kids, lost his job due to reasons totally beyond his control. The bank was about to foreclose on his home. The bank manager, blinded by thirty-five years of following policy, offered no options for his customer. I thought there must be some way to help people with a lapse in income.

And there is an option. A friend of mine, a private lender, helps people keep their homes. And he helped the man and his family stay in their neighbourhood, keep their kids in the same school, and assisted them with moving on with their lives.

I have written this book for self-employed Canadians with equity in residential or commercial real estate who find themselves in a financial squeeze due to credit card, property or income taxes, or line-of-credit overload and arrears. Most often, their bank has declined their financing request or demanded immediate repayment of a loan. The following is intended to offer information and advice to offer these individuals hope and design a path to get them out of financial difficulty.

Let's get started.

CHAPTER 1

Why Did My Bank Decline Me?

● ● ●

IN THIS CHAPTER, YOU WILL learn why your bank declined you. A decline usually boils down to two parameters: your credit and your income.

CREDIT

You have bad credit due to a slow payment history. For example, you are not making minimum credit-card or line-of-credit payments on time, or you are making late payments on a car loan or a loan with fixed payments. Bad credit could also be as a result of a judgement against you for an unpaid loan or you being in collections for an unpaid loan.

Some other reasons for low credit score include a high utilization of credit. For example, your credit limit is $2,000, and you are constantly showing a balance of $1,999. Or you are over your credit limit on a credit card or line of credit.

For a more in-depth study of credit, refer to chapter 7.

Income

Income is a little more complicated. Banks use a formula for determining affordability for a loan. They use two ratios: gross debt service (GDS) and total debt service (TDS). Once you understand these ratios, they are not so intimidating.

Let's start with the GDS. Here's how it works.

Gross Debt Service (GDS) Ratio Calculation

	Yearly	Monthly
Assumptions:		
Household Income	$80,000	$6,667
House Costs:		
Mortgage Payment	$21,600	$1,800
Property Taxes	$2,600	$217
Heat	$900	$75
Total House Costs	$25,100	$2,092
Other debt obligations:		
Car Payment(s)		$600
VISA Card		$250
Master Card		$350
Alimony/Child Support		$700
Total Other:		$1,900

Gross Debt Service (GDS) Ratio

GDS ratio calculates the ratio of basic costs to own the property in comparison with the gross family income.

$$GDS = \frac{\text{Principal and Interest (\$1,800)} + \text{Heat (\$75)} + \text{Property Taxes (\$217)} = \$2,092}{\text{Gross Family Income (\$6,667)}}$$

$$GDS = \frac{\$2,092}{\$6,667}$$

Your gross debt service, or GDS = 31.38 percent

Total Debt Service (TDS) Ratio

TDS ratio takes into account all the basic costs associated with the GDS, along with all other major monthly obligations.

$$TDS = \frac{\text{Principal and Interest (\$1,800)} + \text{Heat (\$75)} + \text{Property Taxes (\$217)} + \text{Other Monthly Obligations (\$1,900)}}{\text{Gross Family Income}}$$

$$TDS = \frac{\$1,800 + \$75 + \$217 + \$1,900}{\$6,667}$$

$$TDS = \frac{\$3,992}{\$6,667}$$

Your total debt service, or TDS = 58.38 percent

GDS/TDS Summary

Most lenders like to see the GDS at or below 39 percent and the TDS at or below 44 percent. So, in this example, the GDS at 31.88 percent is okay, but the TDS is too high at 58 percent. Often one or both ratios are out of line (too high), or there is bad credit. This is where private lending enters the picture.

Banks also use the following to determine what income to use:

1. You will provide information about your salary, as an employment verification letter, a recent paystub, and T4 can verify.
2. For commissioned salespeople, with a base salary plus commission, you will provide all of the above plus two years' worth of Notice of Assessments (NOA) and a summary of your tax return that the Canada Revenue Agency (CRA) sends back to you after filing your taxes. You could also be asked for two years' worth of T4s.
3. For self-employed individuals, banks will ask for the last two years of your NOA, T1 generals, and something to verify you are self-employed, like your articles of incorporation or a business license.

As you can see, your credit and your income play important interrelated roles in determining a bank's criteria for lending out money.

In this chapter, you learned some possible reasons why your bank declined your loan application. In the next chapter, you will discover how much of a private mortgage loan you may be able to qualify for.

Case Study 1: Robert and Sarah's Credit Crunch

Borrowers	James and Sarah
Bank GDS/TDS	342 / 342
Current First Mortgage	$375,000
Home Value	$800,000
Declared Household Income	$20,000
Second Mortgage Request	$120,000
Total Loan to Value	62%
Biggest Challenge	**Income**

Robert was self-employed, and like many self-employed Canadians, he showed very little income on his tax returns. Sarah did some part-time work for cash and spent most of her time managing the household affairs and bringing up two young children.

Robert's self-employment status allows him to deduct expenses not normally allowed to regular employees; therefore his resulting *declared income* is lower compared to a regular employee.

Robert and Sarah had accumulated $75,000 worth of debt on credit cards and a line of credit. It was starting to choke their monthly cash flow. They requested a total loan of $120,000 to pay off all their debts and have some money left over to put into Robert's business. Robert and Sarah really wanted to keep their first mortgage as it had such a fantastic low rate.

Let's look at their numbers to see how it all worked out:

Before	Balance	Monthly Payment
First Mortgage	$375,000	$3,350
Line of Credit	$40,000	$1,200
Bank Credit Card	$15,000	$450
Credit Union Credit Card	$10,000	$300
Total **Before** Payments		$5,300
Transaction Costs:		
Appraisal	$500	
Legal Lender	$1,200	
Independent Legal Advice	$800	
Broker fee	$4,950	
Lender fee	$4,950	
Working capital required	$42,600	
Total Loan Required	$120,000	
After		
First Mortgage	$375,000	$3,350
Second Mortgage	$120,000	$1,400
Total **After** Payments		$4,750
Savings per month	$550	

Summary

Robert and Sarah were able to pay off all their high-interest debts, which ranged from 18 to 29 percent. They freed themselves from the mandatory, intolerable minimum payments that their bank required and walked away with $42,600 in cash. Robert was able to invest this into his business and save over $550 per month. They have created $550 per month in extra breathing room and now only have two payments to worry about. You can imagine their relief when it was all said and done.

This was the fresh start they had dreamed about and the one their bank could not help them with.

CHAPTER 2

How Much Money Can I Get?

● ● ●

IN THIS CHAPTER, YOU WILL discover what size of private mortgage you may be able to qualify for. For most private lenders, how much money you can borrow depends on how much equity you have in your residential or commercial real estate.

The equity in your properties, your income, and your credit score will determine how much money you can borrow. These answers will help us determine an amount you can afford and for which you are qualified.

Often, we are asked the following:

- Is there any way we can borrow more than we would qualify for at a bank?
- Can I borrow money with no income verification?
- Why can't I get more?

Private lenders rely more on the equity you have in your property than your income or credit score. They will lend up to a certain percentage of your property's value.

Question: Can I get a loan for the same value of my house/commercial property?

The short answer is no. To use simple numbers, let's say your home is worth $100,000. Eighty percent of that is $80,000, the maximum loan amount most private lenders would lend on a home worth $100,000.

In rural areas, many lenders will only go up to 65 percent of the value of the property. Therefore, in the example above, on the property appraised at $100,000, the maximum loan in a rural area could be $65,000.

Question: Why can't I get more than these amounts in the examples above?

The lender needs to have equity behind him or her. In other words, the lender wants to make sure if, in the unlikely event that the loan is not paid and he or she has to sell your home (a foreclosure or power of sale), money will be left over to pay for the loan as well as the cost to go through the process of selling the home.

Sometimes borrowers want a line of credit to pay off their debts. This is not available from a private lender. Typically, a debt consolidation loan is a fixed loan amount that a borrower pays down with monthly fixed payments. Most often, a lender will arrange a loan that will pay out all your debts. This loan will consolidate all your previous debts into one debt with a more manageable payment.

However, beware of your banker! Depending on who the lender is, the more money he or she lends you, the more money and commissions he or she makes.

Are you wondering what kind of debts you can pay off? That's a good question. Most types of debt can be paid off in a consolidation loan, for example, income or property tax arrears, credit-card loans, lines of credit, car loans, and, of course, mortgages.

If you are self-employed and you owe Goods & Services Tax (GST), Harmonized Sales Tax (HST), or other source deductions, those may be included in your loan as well.

Do you wonder what kinds of debts you may not want to pay off? You may have debt that has a very low interest rate and low minimum monthly payments. You may want to keep these loans. There are, however, some loans that have low interest rates but shockingly high minimum-payment requirements, and this is what can adversely affect cash flow. Often these loans are included in the consolidation loan.

Dirty Banker Secret #1
Make no mistake. When you get a mortgage from your banker, he or she is often compensated on how much you borrow! Many borrowers just assume that their banker is on salary. That's not always so!

If you qualify for a $500,000 loan but really only need $400,000, the banker will still encourage you to borrow the entire $500,000 because he or she gets paid on the amount you borrow. This is not always what is in your best interest. What you qualify for and what you can afford are often two different things. For example, when the banker qualifies you, he or she may not take into account that you have children. That's not part of the qualifying process. Often, childcare expenses can be the same price as a mortgage payment. You have to be careful. What you qualify for and what you can afford can be two very different things.

Your banker will also try to get you to take other products he or she is selling. In the industry, it's called *cross-selling*. Bankers want you to take their outrageously high credit-card and line-of-credit products that eventually choke you to death financially with the unbearable minimum-payment requirements and villainous interest rates.

In this chapter, you discovered how much money a private lender may be willing to lend you, and in the next chapter, you will learn all about payments.

Case Study 2: Peter's Investment Emergency

Borrower	Peter
Bank GDS/TDS	*Tilt!*
Current First Mortgage	$0
Home Value	$1,000,000
Declared Household Income	$20,000
Second Mortgage Request	$900,000
Total Loan to Value	90%
Biggest Challenge	**Needed Money Now!**

Peter was a nonresident to Canada. He showed very little income on his tax return and needed almost $1 million in just a few days. Peter owned several other properties that were up for sale as he was liquidating his Canadian real-estate portfolio. Peter needed the money within five days as he was making an overseas investment, and the opportunity was about to expire if he didn't get the money right away. Peter's credit was great. The challenges, however, were as follows: timing/speed, income, residency, and property already listed for sale.

Very few lenders can get almost $1 million out the door on such short notice. Additionally, Peter needed a loan worth 90 percent of the value of his property. No bank in Canada could do this loan. Additionally, as Peter was a nonresident, there would be a 25 percent withholding tax once the property was sold. That meant, if the property sold for $1 million, on closing, only $750,000 would be left over to pay back the loan, a shortfall of $250,000 unless Peter paid the taxes in advance before closing, which is what he did. Of course, real-estate commission and legal expenses also have to be taken into account.

One last challenge is that many lenders will not lend on a property that is currently listed for sale.

Summary

The issue here was complicated due to the various challenges involved: timing, income, residency, and the fact that the property was already listed on the multiple listing service (MLS).

Peter sold his property about ninety days after receiving the loan, paid back the lender in full, and was able to get his definition of a *fresh start* overseas.

Sometimes, situations arise where money is needed very quickly under extenuating circumstances. This was one of them.

CHAPTER 3

What Will My Payment Be?

• • •

IN THIS CHAPTER, I'LL SHARE with you how payments are made on your private mortgage. Your payment will be based on the loan amount. Obviously the higher the loan amount, the higher the payment. Once we know exactly what your loan amount is, then we can calculate a payment for you. There are formulas for that. Check out *the Debt Miracle* in chapter 10.

CAN I PAY ANYTHING, ANYTIME, DURING THE MONTH?
That's a great question. Typically, a consolidation loan (private mortgage) payment is made on the first of every month. Private lenders will have a number of these loans. If each loan has a different payment date, it really complicates bookkeeping for the lender. Unlike a large bank, they don't typically have sophisticated computer and automatic withdrawal systems in place. These loans are set up where the borrower simply issues twelve postdated cheques.

Can I pay every two weeks?

Many borrowers currently pay their first mortgage every two weeks or biweekly. Debt consolidation loans by private lenders are typically payable on the first of each month.

Can I pay it off early if I have the money?

When private lenders provide a loan for somebody, they cannot lend out the money one week and then have it paid back the next. They wouldn't make any money; it's not profitable for them. It has to do with the lender getting an expected yield (interest rate earned) or profit on the money that they're lending out. If the loan is just for a week, two weeks, or a month, that doesn't work for them, so they typically won't do it. If you do pay it out early, there's typically some kind of penalty provision like a three-month interest penalty.

You might be able to negotiate what is called an **open mortgage**, meaning it can be paid out in full at any time during the term of the mortgage. This type of open mortgage may come with a higher interest rate or a minimum three-month term before the loan can be paid out.

Why is there a penalty if I pay it off early?

Paying off the mortgage early means the lender didn't get the full investment return the person was expecting, so it makes the loan unprofitable for him or her. So, if the mortgage is paid out early and the investor/lender doesn't get the person's full return, a three-month penalty gives him or her an acceptable return on his or her money while the person looks for a new investment.

Some lenders promise a certain return to the investor/lender. This is known as *matching*. The penalty might be the balance of interest left on the loan. For example, if the loan term were one year and the borrower wanted to pay it back after eight months, he would have to also repay the four months of remaining interest.

Dirty Banker Secret #2
This is similar to when you hear about a bank charging unspeakable penalties to some of its best customers when they break a mortgage to move to another home.

Depending on your circumstances, it is important to discuss up front how and when the loan will be repaid. Lenders always want to know their exit strategy; in other words, how are they going to get their money back and when? A lender is as concerned with the return *of* its investment as it is with the return *on* its investment!

WHY IS THE MINIMUM TERM ONE YEAR?
Similar to paying a loan off early, when investors or private lenders provide a loan for somebody, they cannot put the money out one week only to have it paid back the next. It's not profitable for them.

Lenders almost always want a one-year investment. Under special circumstances, you might be able to find a lender to do a shorter term.

Can I pay extra on the mortgage?

You want to pay extra. For example, if the minimum payment is $500 per month, you want to pay an extra $200 that month.

Most small lenders do not use complex or advanced software to track their mortgage investments, so paying an extra $200 one month may seem like a simple thing to do. However, it changes the outstanding balance and that in turn changes all the math surrounding the loan. While some may allow it, don't expect it to be the norm.

What about an amortized loan versus an interest-only loan?

Some borrowers often say, "I don't want to pay only the interest. I would like to pay down the balance a bit with each payment." Paying down the balance a little with each payment is technically known as an amortized loan, like the one you would get with your bank, say a twenty-five-year amortization.

Most private lenders offer what's known as an *interest-only loan*. The reason for this is that often borrowers are looking for the lowest possible payment and an interest-only loan meets that requirement. Additionally, in the first half of an amortized loan, very little principal is repaid. It's mostly interest. As private loans are only a year or two in length, there is little advantage in making it an amortized loan.

WHAT IS THE TERM? OR HOW LONG IS THE LOAN FOR?
The term is the period of time that the mortgage is in place for. A typical term is one year. After one year, the lender expects to be paid back. Sometimes, one year is not enough for the borrower to be in a position to pay back the mortgage. If the mortgage were paid as agreed and is in good standing, the lender may extend the mortgage for another year for a renewal fee.

It is important to remember that lenders make their money charging lender fees. That is why they charge a renewal fee for a loan extension. Charging a renewal fee is good for the borrower. It saves the cost of repeating the approval process again. For example, if a new lender were needed, there would need to be a new broker fee, lender fee, legal fees, and possibly appraisal.

You should expect most private lenders to offer a one-year term. If you need more than a one-year term, expect to pay a renewal fee. This could be added to the loan balance. Your mortgage broker can help you determine when you will be ready to repay the private loan with a bank loan.

While your mortgage broker cannot *guarantee* you a period of time, he should be able to give you a rough guideline.

What kind of rate can I expect?

This is a very difficult question to answer until your mortgage broker and the lender know all the details of the loan. Answers to the following questions will determine the rate:

- What is the borrower's credit like?
- How much is his property worth?
- What is the size of the existing mortgage?
- Does the borrower have income that allows him to make the regular monthly payments on the new loan and other existing mortgages?

If the borrower doesn't have enough income, it is still possible to get a loan. It's considered an equity loan rather than an income-qualified loan. This means the lender is willing to lend money based on the equity in the property rather than the borrower's ability to make monthly payments.

An equity loan would only be used in circumstances whereby both the lender and the borrower have a clear exit strategy (repayment of the loan) and determine how the borrower will make the monthly payments.

For example, a borrower wants to do some renovations to his home and then sell it for a profit. A major factor in the rate is the loan to value (LTV), the percentage of the loan relative to the property value. If a property worth $100,000 has a loan of $50,000, it would have an LTV of 50 percent. This is a low-risk loan, and the rate may reflect that. If the total loans on the property were going to be 90 percent, that would be a much riskier loan, and the rate would reflect that.

Dirty Banker Secret #3
Interest rates on private consolidation loans will almost always be less than the horrendous credit-card rates that can be at 18, 19, or even 30 percent. **Beware:** *some well-known institutional lenders will charge the same interest rate on a consolidation loan as they would on a credit card.*

The LTV is a part of the approval process a lender uses to help you decide what debts should be paid out and what debt should stay and ensure that the optimal loan amount is set up to help you pay off your debts and eventually eliminate them.

In this chapter, you discovered how your payments are made on a private mortgage loan. In the next chapter, you will learn how self-employed borrowers go about obtaining a private mortgage.

Case Study 3: Katherine and David's Tears of Joy

Borrowers	Katherine and Dave
Bank GDS/TDS	**28 / 85**
Current First Mortgage	$350,000
Home Value	$785,000
Declared Household Income	$95,000
Second Mortgage Request	$75,000
Total Loan to Value	54%
Biggest Challenge	**Low Credit Scores**

One of the most memorable times was when I was asked what will be the payments. A couple were in tears when they saw the difference between their total minimum payment required for their bank debt (credit cards and lines of credit) and their new second mortgage payment.

They needed a short-term private mortgage to pay off their bank debts.

Somehow, they had managed to make all their minimum payments on time. The only thing holding down their credit scores was the high utilization of their credit (see chapter 7 regarding the credit bureau).

In other words, once the debt was paid off, their credit scores would rise. Their low credit scores were the only thing keeping them from refinancing with a bank.

Insider Secrets About How To Quickly and Easily Pay Off Your Debts

Here's how the numbers unfolded:

Before	Balance	Monthly Payment
First Mortgage	$350,000	$1,646
Lines of Credit (total of 2)	$30,000	$900
Credit Cards (total of 5)	$35,000	$1,050
Total **Before** Payments		$3,596
Transaction Costs:		
Appraisal	$500	
Legal Lender	$1,200	
Independent Legal Advice	$800	
Broker fee	$3,250	
Lender fee	$3,250	
Contingency Funds	$2,000	
Total Funds Required	$76,000	
After		
First Mortgage	$350,000	$1,646
Second Mortgage	$76,000	$862
Total **After** Payments		$2,508
Monthly Savings	**$1,088**	

Summary

Katherine and David had a minimum payment on their bank debt before consolidating of $1,950.00.

With a new second mortgage payment of $862.00, they have a monthly cash-flow savings of $1,088.00.

Assuming Katherine and David take on no new debt and make their mortgage payments on time, within a few months, their credit scores will rise, and they will be able to refinance their first and second mortgages with a bank and save even more.

For example, a new $426,000 first mortgage ($350,000 + $76,000) at 3.25 percent with a twenty-five-year amortization has a monthly payment of $2,071. This is savings of an additional $487 per month.

By taking on the private mortgage to eliminate their nonmortgage debts and with a clear strategy provided by their mortgage broker, Katherine and David wind up with a first mortgage only and savings of $1,575 per month!

Check out *the Debt Miracle* in chapter 10 to see what they can do next.

CHAPTER 4

I'm Self-Employed. Is That Okay?

• • •

IN THIS CHAPTER, YOU WILL discover how self-employed borrowers can qualify and obtain a private mortgage. Some of the most common questions a private lender hears are as follows:

- "I'm self-employed. Is that okay?"
- "Is it okay that I own my own business?"

Yes! If you're self-employed, you might have a sole proprietorship or be incorporated. If you own a business and it's a corporation, that's fine. Or if you're a sole proprietor, that's okay as well.

One thing to keep in mind is that, if you are incorporated, you will still be required to personally sign for the loan. A common misconception is that, because you are incorporated, you will not have to sign personally and guarantee the loan.

I DO SOME CASH BUSINESS. IS THAT ALL RIGHT?
Yes! The main thing that a private lender or a consolidation lender is interested in is the equity in your home or other property, as opposed to your cash flow. They know that, if you are self-employed, you earn money in different ways and often a component of your income is cash.

I'M BEHIND IN FILING MY INCOME TAXES. CAN I STILL GET A LOAN?
Yes! Under most circumstances that will be fine. However, we encourage you to do your taxes, so you know how much is owed. We can actually include those income taxes in your loan so you can have a fresh start.

If you owe income taxes, some lenders may be hesitant to lend because the government can freeze bank accounts and prevent you from making your payments.

I HAVE INCOME TAXES OWING FROM PREVIOUS YEARS. IS THAT OKAY?
Yes! Under most circumstances, back taxes would be one of the first items to be paid out with your new loan, relieving you of the anxiety that owing income taxes can bring.

The CRA is ruthless in collecting income taxes. The CRA can put liens on property, freeze bank accounts, and **seize** items of value.

I have HST/GST or other source deductions owing. Is that all right?

Yes! All lenders would require these to be included in the loan. This type of CRA debt is especially troubling for a lender because, in Canada, these types of debts have priority over everything registered on the title of your home. Even though a mortgage may have been registered long ago and be in "first" position, GST/HST and other source deductions have super priority over that first mortgage. In other words, these debts would rank ahead of any mortgage registered regardless of when it was registered. The government ensures they will be paid first.

The CRA already has a lien on my property. Can you help?

Yes! This will be paid out and included in the loan amount. If you don't do anything about the lien, the CRA's next step could be to force the sale of your property, and you could lose your home.

What if I don't show any income?

No problem! If you don't have verifiable income, like what you would show on a tax return, that's okay as long as you can demonstrate that you have other sources of income and can demonstrate an ability to make the loan payments.

If the borrower doesn't have enough verifiable or other income, there is yet another option. You could qualify for an *equity loan*. This means the lender is willing to lend the money based on the equity in the property rather than the borrower's ability to make monthly payments.

An equity loan would only be used in circumstances whereby both the lender and the borrower have a clear strategy for exit (repayment of the loan) and determine how the borrower will make the payments. An example would be a borrower wants to do some renovations to the property and then sell it for a profit. The exit for the lender would be the sale of the property.

In this chapter, you discovered some of the challenges the self-employed face while obtaining a loan and how to overcome those challenges. In the next chapter, you will learn who the lenders are for private mortgages and how they work.

Case Study 4: Dimitri's Parents

Borrowers	Dimistri's Parents
Bank GDS/TDS	*Way over the top!*
Current First Mortgage	$352,000
Home Value	$500,000
Declared Household Income	$250,000
Second Mortgage Request	$55,000
Total Loan to Value	81%
Biggest Challenge	**Very Little Income**

Dimitri was representing his parents as they spoke no English, had very little income, were halfway through a renovation, and had run out of money. The plan was to finish the renovation and sell the home so Dimitri's parents could have some extra cash as they were long retired and running short of funds.

Let's look at their numbers to see how it all worked out:

Before	Balance	Monthly Payment
First Mortgage	$352,000	$1,532
Total **Before** Payment		$1,532
Transaction Costs:		
Appraisal	$500	
Legal Lender	$1,200	
Indendent Legal Advice	$800	
Broker fee	$2,500	
Lender fee	$2,500	
Renovation Funds	$47,500	
Total Funds Required	$55,000	
After		
First Mortgage	$352,000	$1,532
Second Mortgage	$55,000	$642
Total **After** Payments		$2,174

Summary

This was a case of no bank willing to lend money to an elderly couple with no employment income. The income they had was a small government pension. The private loan helped them complete a partially finished renovation so they could sell their home and free up some cash.

With the loan advanced, Dimitri and his friends helped complete the required renovations. The loan was paid back in full when their newly renovated home sold in just a few days.

Their banker had completely ignored them once it was determined that he couldn't get them approved and make money off them. They were one step away from losing their home. Dimitri's parents were over eighty years old and nearly thrown out into the streets!

They got their fresh start to a worry-free retirement.

CHAPTER 5

Who Is the Lender?

● ● ●

IN THIS CHAPTER, YOU WILL learn who the lenders are for private mortgages and how they work. Many clients ask, "Who are these lenders?"

Lenders range from institutions and mortgage investment corporations (MICs) to private individuals. Typically, the institutional lender (banks, credit unions, trust companies, and so on) is the least expensive.

But most clients seek our help because *their bank turned them down*. After years of charging them interest, sinful banking charges, and often scandalously bad bank service, their bank of years has said no. So much for the valued relationship banks so often talk about. They are happy to lend you an umbrella on a sunny day!

MICs tend to be less flexible than a true private lender. Loan approval is by a credit committee. This can be time consuming. The loan has to meet the requirements of the corporation's offering memorandum (the document containing the policies that determine how loans are approved and made). Although not as bureaucratic as a bank, they are nowhere near **as** *flexible as a private lender*, especially if there is a time constraint. In other words, if the borrower needs the money in a couple of days, a private lender is the best option.

It could be any one of the three. Typically, the solution is a private lender.

I'VE NEVER HEARD OF THAT LENDER. IS THAT OKAY?
Yes! Most private lenders are not known to the general public. They're not household names because they are literally private citizens using their own money to make mortgage investments as a source of income. Some private lenders use their retirement money, or it could be the business they are in.

WHAT IF THE LENDER GOES OUT OF BUSINESS OR GOES BANKRUPT?
A lot of people ask that question, and I always joke and say, "Well, if the lender goes out of business or goes bankrupt and forgets about you, then you've got yourself a free loan [chuckle]." The reality is if that happens, the assets (mortgages) are sold to somebody else, and they will continue to administer the loan.

Additionally, the loan is registered on the title of your property, so when you sell the property, someone has to be paid back.

How do I pay back the lender?
The lender is paid back through a combination of monthly payments and the eventual refinance of the private mortgage into an institutional one. A private mortgage is a temporary solution to a financial problem.

The idea is that it's a two-phased process. First, we consolidate all your debts into one manageable first or second mortgage loan. This will improve your credit. We **coach you** so you are ready to go to an institutional lender (bank) within one to three years of taking out this private loan.

What if I can't pay back the lender?
In the rare circumstance where you can't pay back the lender, you can negotiate for a longer term until you are able to pay him or her back. If there is lots of equity in your property, the lender will probably be okay with that. Alternatively, another lender may have to be found. Under an absolute worst-case scenario, you may have to sell your house to pay back the lender, but this is rare because working with a reputable lender, an exit strategy (how the loan

is to be repaid) would have been considered before making the loan.

In this chapter, you discovered who the lender is, what he or she expects from you, and what you can expect from him or her. In the next chapter, you will learn about appraisals.

Case Study 5: Sean the Contractor

Borrower	Sean The Contractor
Bank GDS/TDS	**60 / 80 Way too high for a bank**
Current First Mortgage	$215,000
Home Value	$855,000
Declared Household Income	$52,000
Second Mortgage Request	$90,000
Total Loan to Value	36%
Biggest Challenge	**Credit**

Sean is self-employed with his own contracting business. He fell behind in filing his income-tax-returns, credit-card, and line-of-credit payments. This damaged his credit. His property taxes were also overdue, which was discovered during the mortgage application process. Further complicating things were a couple of judgements against him totalling $8,700, not discovered until the lender's lawyer did a search to see if Sean had any outstanding judgements he was unaware of. Sean's wife had a full-time salaried job paying $50,000.

The pressure had been mounting for quite some time as the CRA and the city were both looking for their owed taxes. Additionally, Sean's business had lost access to most of its credit due to maxed-out balances. Any new credit Sean applied for was denied due to his low credit score.

The solution was a second mortgage to pay out the income taxes, judgements, property-tax arrears, and credit-card balances. The mortgage had a one-year term with a renewal option to give Sean's credit score some time to recover. At the end of two years, he was able to replace the existing first and second mortgages with a new first mortgage at an overall lower rate. See chapter 7 for a better understanding on how the credit score and the credit bureau works.

Before	Balance	Monthly Payment
First Mortgage	$215,000	$1,510
Lines of Credit (total of 2)	$28,000	$870
Credit Cards (total of 4)	$25,000	$750
Property Tax Arrears	$17,500	
Judgements (total of 2)	$8,700	
Total **Before** Payment		$3,130
Transaction Costs:		
Appraisal	$500	
Legal Lender	$2,000	
Independent Legal Advice	$800	
Broker fee	$3,750	
Lender fee	$3,750	
Total Loan Required	$90,000	
After		
First Mortgage	$215,000	$1,510
Second Mortgage	$90,000	$1,050
Total **After** Payment		$2,560
Monthly Savings	$570	

Summary

With a $90,000 private second mortgage, Sean's income taxes, credit cards, lines of credit, property tax arrears, and judgements were paid off. Transaction costs were covered in the loan amount. Sean and his wife could take a big sigh of relief and get on with their *fresh start*, all the while saving $570 per month from their previous situation.

CHAPTER 6

How Does the Appraisal Work?

● ● ●

IN THIS CHAPTER, WE WILL reveal what you need to know about the appraiser and the appraisal process. The process of consolidating all your debts into one mortgage on your property often requires that the property is appraised.

WHO PAYS FOR THE APPRAISAL?
The borrower pays for the appraisal. The cost can be reimbursed to you as part of the loan proceeds.

WHY DOES THE BORROWER PAY FOR THE APPRAISAL?
If the lender were to pay for the appraisal and the deal did not proceed, the lender would be out of pocket. Appraisals can be negatively affected in many ways as follows:

- Condition of property
- Value of the property comes in too low

- Proximity to a negative feature that affects the property value, like a nuclear power plant
- Property located on a flood plain

And many other factors are in play.

How much is the appraisal?

Appraisal costs can vary significantly depending on the location of the property, property type, and property complexity.

A typical residential appraisal would be in the $300 to $500 range. For a more complex or remote property, it could be as high as $3,000. For a commercial property, appraisals start in the $2,000 range.

What about the value in my Municipal Property Assessment Corporation (MPAC) or property assessment statement?

A question often asked is, "I just received my property tax statement. Can't the lender just use that as the value of the property?"

No. Although the property valuation data is one of the tools that the government uses in the calculation of the property taxes, it rarely corresponds to the market value of a property. It can be higher or lower than the market value.

If the value on the statement is higher than the market value and the lender were to rely on that as the market value, he would be putting his investment at risk. Should the loan ever go into default and the property needed to be sold, there may not be enough money left over to pay back the investor after all the sale costs have been paid.

Conversely, if the value of the property is higher than what the MPAC statement shows, then this will negatively affect the actual loan amount available to the borrower (a lower loan amount). Often the borrower needs the maximum value of his property in order to get the maximum amount of loan to help him with his **fresh start**. The MPAC statement is really only a guide for the municipality to use to calculate your property taxes.

The mortgage broker has a fiduciary duty to the investor in the arrangement of the mortgage to ensure the investor's money is protected against any default.

It is in the best interest of all parties to have a professional appraiser with an Accredited Appraiser Canadian Institute (AACI) designation assess the property.

How does the appraiser come up with the value?

The appraiser evaluates recent home sales in your neighbourhood and compares them to your house. These are called *comparables* in appraiser-speak.

Appraisers use a process to compare your home to others in your neighbourhood, even if they are different than yours. If, for example, the other house has more bathrooms than yours, it will have a slightly higher value than yours. If your house has a finished basement and another house doesn't, then your house will have a slightly higher value than that house and so on. These are known as *adjustments* in appraisal parlance. Comparables will be adjusted upward or down to get an accurate valuation.

A typical appraisal report will be fifteen to twenty pages. It will include property details, specifications, a narrative about the area, maps, pictures of the interior and exterior, and the comparables they used to determine the value of your home.

What if the appraiser is wrong and I don't agree with the value?

Homeowners often overestimate the value of their home. But if you don't agree with the appraiser's value, you can ask for another appraisal. You would have to pay for that additional appraisal as well.

Lenders typically have a list of approved appraisers whose reports they will accept.

Even if you feel the appraisal number is low, there is often enough equity in your home to satisfy the lender and complete the loan. No one truly knows what your home is worth until you sell it on the open market.

Who is the appraiser?

As mentioned, most private lenders have a list of appraisers whose reports they will accept. They will not accept an appraisal supplied by the borrower.

On the lender's approved list, the appraiser will almost always have an Accredited Appraiser Canadian Institute (AACI) designation from the Appraisal Institute of Canada. AACI members are qualified to offer valuation, consulting services, and expertise for all types of real estate property (commercial and residential).

There is another designation called Canadian Residential Appraiser (CRA). CRA members are qualified to offer valuation, consulting services, and expertise for individual, undeveloped residential dwelling sites and dwellings containing not more than four self-contained family housing units.

Most lenders prefer a report prepared by an AACI.

Can I get a copy of the appraisal?

Lenders consider the appraisal an internal document. They don't allow appraisals to be shared publicly with anyone other than those connected to the lending process.

The appraiser's obligation is first and foremost to his client. The client is always the lender, whose instructions the appraisal is prepared under. Even though the borrower pays for the appraisal, the appraiser cannot provide it to the borrower because the borrower is not his client.

The appraisal required by the lender is basically a non-refundable fee, and if the mortgage does not fund, the fee must still be paid, which is why the borrower pays it up front.

If the client directly asks a mortgage broker for a copy of the appraisal report, the experienced broker will first ask for the lender's approval. It is rarely granted.

A mortgage broker providing an appraisal to a borrower risks personal legal liability.

A professional mortgage broker would never put himself or his client in that position.

What if the appraiser doesn't know my neighbourhood?

If the appraiser is not familiar with your neighbourhood, there's a good chance that he will inform the lender, and another appraiser will be chosen. The appraiser has a professional duty to only perform appraisals he can competently complete. To do otherwise, the appraiser risks possible litigation. And what appraiser would want that?

My house is the only one with a finished basement and has the largest lot on the street. Will that help my value?

Yes. If your house is the only one with a finished basement and has the largest lot, then it will appraise higher than a similar house in the area with a smaller lot and no finished basement. Refer to *comparables* and *adjustments* previously discussed in this chapter.

Do I have to be there while the appraisal is being done?

Yes. You have to be there because the appraiser is going to come into your home or other property, take a few pictures and some measurements, and then leave. Also, you will want to be on hand to answer any questions the appraiser might have that could affect his assessment of how your property is valued.

Do I have to prepare or clean my residential or commercial property for the appraiser?

You don't have to, but it's like anything else. It is better if your property is clean, neat, and tidy, inside and out. A presentable-looking property will likely appraise higher than the same in a filthy state.

Think of Christmastime under the Christmas tree. There are two gifts under the tree, and both are the exact same gift. One is wrapped in newspaper, the other one is wrapped in really nice paper with a bow on it. You're going to want the one with the nice wrapping. While it's not necessary, and theoretically it should not affect the value of your property, a clean one will likely appraise higher than a filthy one. Appraisers are only human.

I have an appraisal that was done six months ago. Can I provide that one?

No. Appraisals are considered stale if they're older than sixty days. A new one will be required. Market conditions can change quickly. A prudent appraiser would caution against using any appraisal older than sixty days, including his own.

In this chapter, you have discovered all you will need to know about the appraiser and the appraisal process. In the next chapter, you will learn about the credit bureau and how to fix your bad credit.

Case Study 6: Tim's Start-up

Borrower	Tim's Start Up
Bank GDS/TDS	*Off the charts*
Current First Mortgage	$1,000,000
Home Value	$1,700,000
Declared Household Income	$40,000
Second Mortgage Request	$250,000
Total Loan to Value	74%
Biggest Challenge	Income

Five years ago, Tim created an innovative software start-up that required some additional funds to keep it going. He had ongoing expenses like paying third-party software developers, rent, and overhead associated with operating a business. His start-up was close to, but not yet, generating any revenue.

With no real verifiable income, Tim's best option was a private second mortgage on his principal residence. And he needed the money fast as creditors were pounding on his door for payment.

Here's how the numbers unfolded:

Before	Balance	Monthly Payment
First Mortgage	$1,000,000	$2,900
Total **Before** Payments		$2,900
Transaction Costs:		
Appraisal	$500	
Legal Lender	$1,200	
Independent Legal Advice	$800	
Broker fee	$5,000	
Lender fee	$20,000	
Working Capital	$222,500	
Total Loan Required	$250,000	
After		
First Mortgage	$1,000,000	$2,900
Second Mortgage	$250,000	$2,500
Total **After** Payments		$5,400

Summary

Tim's situation was not about improving cash flow. It was about needing money quickly to meet the demands of his start-up expenses. Tim's first mortgage was an interest-only payment, which helped keep his overall payments low. His bank of many years, of course, refused his request for help.

After arranging a $250,000 private second mortgage, including all the fees and costs associated with setting it up, Tim was able to return his focus to his start-up and devote all his attention to its success.

CHAPTER 7

What If I Have Bad Credit?

• • •

IN THIS CHAPTER, YOU WILL learn the secrets of the credit bureau. We will discuss how it works and how you can improve your bad score or make your good score better.

Bad credit is not a problem. That's why we're here. We are here to help you improve your credit. If you have enough equity in your home, we can create a strategy for your successful fresh start. Your credit becomes a nonissue.

How does the credit bureau work?

Credit scores range from 300 to 900. These are theoretical minimum and maximum credit score values. The higher the score, the better the credit is considered. Someone with a credit score of 300 is basically on life support. I've never seen a score that low. On the other hand, someone like Warren Buffett probably doesn't have the theoretical maximum 900 score either.

Often, well-to-do people don't have very good credit scores. They sometimes also need private debt consolidation loans because they don't qualify at their own bank due to a low credit score.

A credit score below 600 is considered low. In Canada, it's tough to get a mortgage at one of the six big banks with a score below 600. Canada Mortgage and Housing Corporation (CMHC) will not insure loans where the borrower has a score below this number.

For self-employed individuals, the minimum score is 650. Some lenders require 680. For premium products or a very low rate, some lenders like to see self-employed individuals with scores greater than 720.

These are the *four secrets* you need to know about the credit bureau. (I'll explain each in more detail.)

1. Pay on time.
2. Minimize inquiries.
3. Keep utilization less than 50 percent.
4. Pay off judgements/collections now.

Credit-Bureau Secret #1: Pay on Time

Late payments are one of the most challenging things to overcome on your credit bureau. The only thing that can fix late payment history is time itself. Payment patterns get the most weighting for the past eighteen to twenty-four months, so recent late payments can really lower a score. It's like the old Chinese proverb, "The best time to plant a tree was twenty-five years ago; the second-best time is now."

Starting today, pay all your bills on time. In the case of credit-card and line-of-credit payments, you don't have to pay off the whole thing each month if you can't. For starters, just *always* make the minimum required payment on time.

The strategy is this: two years from now, you will apply for bank financing to repay your consolidation loan. The new loan will attract a lower interest rate. The lender will see that the slow payment history was twenty-four months ago, and since then, everything has been paid on time. They will appreciate the change from slow payer to prompt payer. Believe it or not, lenders do like a story about why there was bad credit and will take that into account when deciding on a loan.

Credit-Bureau Secret #2: Minimize Inquiries

An inquiry to the credit bureau is made every time you apply for credit. These are known as *hits* to your credit bureau and are also known as *hard inquiries*. Hard inquiries affect your credit score. Soft inquiries do not. We will discuss the difference between hard and soft inquiries.

The story: you go to a car dealership, a motorcycle dealership, a marina, a furniture store, and a credit card, and apply for loans at all these places. With so many different hard inquiries to the credit bureau, this will hurt your score.

How much it hurts depends on what your credit-bureau score was to begin with. For example, if you have a really high credit score now, let's say in the 800s, and you have a bunch of inquiries, it may have little or no effect on your score. It may drop from 810 to 805, which in the world of credit scores is essentially the same great score.

However, if your score is currently 605 and then you get all these hard inquiries, your score could drop by 30 points to 575. Any score below 600 makes bank financing a lot more challenging, if not impossible. *Don't apply for credit unless you absolutely have to.*

An advantage to dealing with a mortgage broker is that he or she will pull your credit score once. He will use that report when dealing with various lenders, saving many unnecessary hits or hard inquiries to your credit bureau. As you now know, this can be a critical strategy when looking to consolidate your debts and getting that *fresh start.*

So, when you go to a major department store at Christmastime and they offer you 20 percent off everything in the store if you sign up for one of their credit cards, think twice before taking them up on the offer.

CREDIT-BUREAU SECRET #3: KEEP UTILIZATION LESS THAN 50 PERCENT

What the hell does this mean? Let's say you have a credit card with a $10,000 limit. The idea here is that, if you carry a balance on your credit card, try to keep that balance below $5,000. Spending $5,000 on a credit card with a $10,000 limit is 50 percent utilization. This level of utilization will not typically degrade your credit score.

Let's say you have another credit card with a $10,000 limit and you always carry a balance of $9,950. That is 99.5 percent utilization of credit and will negatively impact your score. *Never allow your balance to exceed your credit limit. This will slay your credit score!* The same thing can be said for lines of credit.

Your current credit score has an impact on how the various levels of utilization will affect your score. Someone with a really high credit score may not be as affected by an 85 percent utilization of a credit card or line of credit. Someone with slow payments and a low credit score will experience a significant decrease in his score with 85 percent utilization.

Credit-Bureau Secret #4: Pay Off Judgement/Collections Now

Any judgements or collections showing on the credit bureau should be paid off immediately. These really hurt your credit score.

An example I often give is this. You get into a dispute with your cell-phone company over what you perceive to be a fifty-dollar overcharge on your phone bill. The wrong thing to do is refuse to pay it and ignore their demands for payment.

Years or months later when you go to apply for a loan, your credit score will show that there's a collection or judgement against you for fifty dollars. You just slashed your credit over fifty dollars. The best thing to do is to pay the fifty dollars and then dispute with the phone company later.

What's the difference between a consumer proposal and bankruptcy?

A *consumer proposal* is a process during which you make a new arrangement with your unsecured creditors (credit that doesn't have collateral attached to it) for a monthly payment you can afford. An example of an unsecured creditor would be a credit card or a line of credit. Secured creditors, such as your car loan or your home mortgage, are not part of the proposal unless you are willing to give up the asset.

To qualify for a consumer proposal, your debts cannot exceed $250,000, excluding the mortgage on your principal residence. A secured credit line is one in which the borrower uses an asset like a car or a home as collateral to secure the loan. The lender can seize the asset if the borrower doesn't repay the debt according to the terms. Creditors usually offer lower interest rates, higher spending limits, and better terms on secured lines of credit.

Unsecured lines of credit require no collateral. A creditor is accepting the borrower's word that he will repay the debt. It usually is difficult to get an unsecured line of credit approved unless you are a well-established business or an individual with an excellent credit rating.

Credit cards are the most common form of unsecured lines of credit. If you don't repay an unsecured debt, the lender may hire a debt collector or sue to collect the debt.

Bankruptcy is a legal proceeding available to help a person overcome a financial burden he is no longer able to handle. Bankruptcy legislation gives a person overwhelmed with debt the chance to be relieved of that debt and start over. To file for bankruptcy, a person has to be insolvent. The criterion for insolvency is a person shall owe at least $1,000. Also, he is not able to meet his debts when they are due to be paid.

What affects my credit score?

The four credit-bureau secrets are the big drivers of your credit score. You may want to go over them again to make sure you've got it. Pay on time. Minimize inquiries. Keep utilization below 50 percent. Pay off judgements/collections now.

How can I improve my score?

There are many reasons that somebody has a low score. Most often, it's late payments or high utilization. You can improve your score in several ways. The hardest part to repair is a low score due to late payments, because it takes the longest to disappear from your credit-bureau report.

Specifically, it takes eighteen to twenty-four months for late payments to lessen the impact on your credit score.

Decrease utilization. Do not exceed 50 percent of your available credit limit. If your only issue is limits, shortly after paying off all your debts, your credit score will jump significantly.

Your credit score will suffer greatly from credit cards, lines of credit, or debts that are shown as *written off* on the credit bureau. Unsatisfied (not paid off) judgements also greatly affect your score. Once you pay off the judgements, your credit score will improve.

How long does a derogatory item stay on my credit bureau?

Late payments (a type of derogatory item on your credit bureau) will stay on the report for years, but their greatest effect lasts eighteen to twenty-four months. Consumer proposals and bankruptcies remain on the credit bureau for about seven years.

Dirty Banker Secret #4

If you chose not to make any payments on a credit card or line of credit, chances are the bank will eventually report to the credit bureau that debt has been written off. This can stay on the credit bureau for up to seven years.

It is important to note that, if any payments are made to that debt, the seven years starts over again from the date the last payment was received.

How do I contact the credit bureau?

The two most popular consumer credit bureaus in Canada are Equifax and TransUnion. Both are huge bureaucracies and don't have the best customer service. They don't consider you their customer. Their customers are the big banks and other lenders that report to them.

The best way to contact the credit bureau is to look up their contact information on the web.

What if something on my credit-bureau report is wrong?

You can contact the credit bureau in question and have the item corrected or, in rare circumstances, deleted. If you need to, it takes time to correct or update something on the credit bureau. Be sure to have all the supporting documentation ready. The credit bureau won't just take you at your word.

In this chapter, you have learned about the major aspects of the credit bureau, how it works, how to keep a great score, and which steps to take to improve a bad score.

Case Study 7: Jay's Partner Buyout

Borrowers	Jay and his wife
Bank GDS/TDS	*75 / 120*
Current First Mortgage	$450,000
Home Value	$750,000
Declared Household Income	$25,000
Second Mortgage Request	$55,000
Total Loan to Value	67%
Biggest Challenge	**Income**

Jay had been in a business partnership for seven years. It contained a shotgun (buyout) clause. Jay ended up having to buy his partner's half of the company, and he needed the money within five days.

Here's how the numbers unfolded:

Before	Balance	Monthly Payment
First Mortgage	$450,000	$2,247
Total **Before** Payment		$2,247
Transaction Costs:		
Appraisal	$500	
Legal Lender	$1,200	
Independent Legal Advice	$800	
Broker fee	$2,000	
Lender fee	$3,000	
Buyout Funds	$47,500	
Total Funds Required	$55,000	
After		
First Mortgage	$450,000	$2,247
Second Mortgage	$55,000	$624
Total **After** Payments		$2,871

Summary

Jay required the buyout money on very short notice. His long-time banker friend had said he could help. After three months of back and forth, his banker finally told him that he wouldn't be of any help after all. Jay lacked verifiable income (didn't show enough income on his tax return). When Jay and the banker first talked about it, his banker buddy knew his income was low but he had equity in his home. It is a common scenario for a banker to string along a client, telling him that he can get a loan approved that doesn't fit bank guidelines. If time is tight and your deal is in jeopardy, take a private loan and pay it out later if somehow the banker comes through.

After arranging a $55,000 private second mortgage, Jay was able to pay out his problematic partner and include all the transaction costs in the second mortgage. The only money Jay had to come up with was the appraisal cost. A short time later, Jay was able to pay out his first and second mortgage from financing we arranged for him with a different bank.

CHAPTER 8

What Are the Costs Involved?

• • •

IN THIS CHAPTER, I WILL share with you the costs associated with consolidating your debt into a mortgage so you can start moving toward your *fresh start* with confidence and satisfaction.

There are costs involved in obtaining a second mortgage—legal fees, lender fees, broker fees, and an appraisal. That's it.

WHO PAYS THESE COSTS?
The costs are borne by the borrower. Remember, the investor is all about getting a return on his money, not about spending it.

WHAT IS THE BROKER FEE?
The mortgage broker charges the broker fee to find the investor with the money willing to help you with your fresh start.

What does the mortgage broker do?

Many mortgage brokers actually have little or no access to this type of investor as their specialty is dealing with banks and other AAA or prime lenders. The mortgage broker may have family members, lifelong relationships, other relationships, or even himself as a potential lender for you.

Some will tell you right away that it is not their line of work. Others may try to find you the money even though it is not their specialty. This is typically true of new and inexperienced brokers who are low on money and really need to earn a commission. It takes years to develop relationships with various private investors who will do these types of loans.

Investors have minimum and maximum loan amounts. They also have maximum LTV (see chapter 3) they are willing to go to. Investors can be very picky about the geographic region they will lend in. Some will only lend in the Greater Toronto Area (GTA). Others will not lend in the GTA and prefer to lend only in the region in which they know or live.

A private mortgage cannot be obtained in Ontario without the use of a mortgage broker to facilitate the loan. It's the law. A mortgage broker is a licensed professional who has to meet a code of ethics and have his license renewed every two years. Only after confirming that he has met continuing education requirements and not run afoul of the law can he renew his license.

The mortgage broker starts by taking your application and inputting it into software designed to organize the information and share it with potential lenders. The mortgage broker is required to do a lot of due diligence work and often has an administrative team to help arrange the mortgage.

The next step is for the mortgage broker to prepare what is known as a loan package for the investors he or she feels may be interested in the loan. The mortgage broker will make preliminary calls to investors he or she feels would have interest in the investment. The mortgage broker will send the loan package to interested investors for their review.

The loan package often includes the following:

- The applicant's mortgage application
- A copy of the credit bureau
- The applicant's income verification
- A copy of the appraisal
- Pictures of the property
- A narrative of the borrower's situation and why he or she needs the loan
- The exit strategy for the investor
- Why the mortgage broker thinks this is a good investment
- The suitability of the loan for the applicant
- A list of the debts and related statements to be paid out
- A list of the debts that will remain
- A copy of what's currently on the title of the property

Once a suitable investor has been found and has agreed to fund the loan, the broker is required by law to prepare an investor-disclosure statement for the investor. The investor-disclosure statement is known in Ontario as a Form 1 and is a thirteen-page, exhaustive form outlining for the investor all the details about the borrower and the property. Once the investor has signed the investor-disclosure statement, the mortgage broker can prepare the regulatory disclosure documents required for the borrower.

At this point, the borrower is required to sign the borrower disclosure statement as well as the application, the lender commitment, an amortization schedule, and any other documents the mortgage broker feels are pertinent to the transaction. The loan is now ready to be handed over to lawyers.

In Ontario, private mortgages require the use of two lawyers. One lawyer acts for the lender; the other lawyer acts for the borrower. This is called *Independent Legal Advice* (ILA). The borrower requires ILA so he is fully aware and advised about the loan and the consequences for failing to meet the obligations of the loan. A private mortgage loan cannot proceed without the borrower receiving ILA. As stated earlier, the borrower pays for the costs of both these lawyers.

Once all the legal disclosures have been completed, the mortgage is ready to fund. The mortgage broker will help coordinate the transfer of the funds from the lender to the lender's lawyer's trust account. One of the lawyers is tasked with paying out the borrower's debts. It could be either one depending on what was agreed to ahead of time.

The mortgage broker will also provide the lawyer copies of credit-card, line-of-credit, or other loan statements to be paid out and to verify the amount owing as well as account numbers.

It is very important for the mortgage broker to have the current statements and documentation of the debts being paid out so the correct accounts are paid out. It is a rookie mistake for the mortgage broker or the lawyers to accept verbal account numbers and balances owing. A good broker will only accept current statements.

The borrower's lawyer, the one providing the ILA, will receive the funds from the lender's lawyer. After all the agreed-upon debts are paid out and there remains a surplus of funds left over, the lawyer will forward these to the borrower.

Sometimes the borrower will receive excess funds as a result of the loan; other times, they will not. This is because the loan may have been arranged for just enough to pay all the costs and the debts with no additional funds going to the borrower. Other times, the borrower may be paying off debts and still have enough equity in his home to borrow additional funds. They will be free to do what they wish with these surplus funds, such as complete a renovation, buy a car, and so on.

What is a lender fee?

A lender fee is a fee charged by the lender in addition to the stated interest rate on the loan. All private lenders charge a lender fee. They need a return on their investment as well as compensation for the overhead associated with running a private lending business.

Can these costs be included in the loan amount?

Yes! Often all these costs can be included in the loan amount. The borrower will not be required to come up with any up-front costs, with the exception of the appraisal and possibly a retainer fee for the lawyers. If there is sufficient room in the loan amount, the borrower could have all costs associated with the mortgage transaction paid for out of the proceeds.

Are there any hidden costs?

No, a good broker will not hide any costs. The mortgage broker is required to disclose all the costs involved in the transaction in the borrower disclosure form.

On occasion, a lien or a writ of execution could be registered on title unbeknownst to the borrower. As we learned in chapter 5, "Sean the Contractor," these liens or writs of execution take precedence over any new mortgage charges. These must be paid out before any new mortgage charges can be registered on the title. The cost of paying out these liens or writs can be included in the loan amount. This may require a larger loan or may mean that some other debts will remain unpaid.

These liens or writs of execution are often discovered when the lender's lawyer, as part of his or her due diligence process, does a search on the title of the property. This would be an example of an unexpected cost rather than a hidden one.

How long does it take to get the money?

In a perfect world, it can be done in a day! However, this is very rare. The cost is often prohibitive as lawyers would probably triple their fees, as would the other players involved in the transaction. The sooner the money is required, the more expensive it is.

Under normal circumstances, one to three weeks is a good estimate of the time it takes to process a private mortgage. Keep in mind that one week is still a very tight time frame.

Often, funding is delayed due to the borrower not providing documents requested in a timely manner. Lawyers can also slow down the process due to their current workload. Of course, a mortgage broker would never be the cause of a delayed loan!

In this chapter, you have learned the costs associated with arranging a private mortgage. In the next chapter, you will discover how the legal side of things work in private mortgage lending.

Case Study 8: Victor's Illness Kills His Credit

Borrowers	Victor and Susan
Bank GDS/TDS	***30 / 35***
Current First Mortgage	$420,000
Home Value	$635,000
Declared Household Income	$122,000
Second Mortgage Request	$62,000
Total Loan to Value	76%
Biggest Challenge	**Low Credit Scores**

Victor and Susan are a happily married couple of twenty-plus years. They both had great careers with well-paying jobs. Then came Victor's sudden stroke. As a result of suddenly losing Victor's income and facing substantial medical and rehabilitation costs not covered by the health-care system, Victor and Susan's credit started feeling the pinch.

Here's what the numbers looked like:

Before	Balance	Monthly Payment
First Mortgage	$420,000	$2,396
Lines of Credit (total of 2)	$33,000	$1,450
Credit Cards (total of 3)	$19,000	$570
Total **Before** Payments		$4,416
Transaction Costs:		
Appraisal	$500	
Legal Lender	$1,200	
Independent Legal Advice	$800	
Broker fee	$2,750	
Lender fee	$2,750	
Contingency Funds	$2,000	
Total Funds Required	$62,000	
After		
First Mortgage	$420,000	$2,396
Second Mortgage	$62,000	$725
Total **After** Payments		$3,121
Monthly Savings	$1,295	

Summary

As you can see from the GDS/TDS ratios, Victor and Susan would have no problem making the payment on a refinance of their first mortgage to pay off all their debts. Their formerly friendly banker of ten years refused to help even after Victor and Susan explained the reason for their challenges. Their banker said, "Sorry. Your credit is not good enough." He offered no help when they needed it most.

Ironically, after paying off bank credit cards and bank lines of credit with a private mortgage, their monthly cash flow improved significantly! A $62,000 private second mortgage was arranged that paid off *all* their debts and all the transaction costs. Victor and Susan were able to get their fresh start. This allowed Victor to recover from his stroke without the worry of paying bills. The only cost of the financing that Victor and Susan had to come up with was the cost of the appraisal.

The plan is to refinance the first and second mortgages into a new first mortgage once Victor and Susan's credit has recovered. This should take about one year.

Note the huge monthly cash-flow savings of $1,295 after the second mortgage financing was complete.

CHAPTER 9

Why Is There a Lawyer Involved?

● ● ●

IN THIS CHAPTER, YOU WILL learn about how the lawyers are integrated into the private mortgage process. In Ontario, when securing any kind of mortgage, a lawyer is the only one who can register that security on the title of the property. In private lending, there are always two lawyers involved, one for the borrower and one for the lender.

HOW MUCH ARE THE LEGAL FEES?
Legal fees are typically around $1,500 on the lender side, and the ILA by the second lawyer is typically around $800. I don't like to quote legal fees because I'm not a lawyer, but those are typically what they are as of the writing and publishing of this book. If the financing is complicated and requires extra work, the fees could be higher.

Extra work could mean

- defects on the title of the property that have to be cleaned up;
- unexpected liens registered against the title of the property;
- unexpected writs of execution;
- ownership of property in a corporation; or
- a host of other possibilities.

Who pays the legal fees?

As stated earlier, the borrower pays for the costs of both these lawyers.

Why does the borrower pay for both the lawyers' fees?

You may recall from previous chapters that the investor/lender does not incur any cost. Lenders are helping you solve a problem. The borrower is obligated to pay for all the costs of solving his or her own problems. The lender expects a return on his or her investment. Any cost to the lender to do this would not make it worthwhile.

What is ILA?

As mentioned previously, when applying for an institutional loan from a bank, the government allows for only one lawyer to be involved. When there is a private lender involved, the government and the law society require that two lawyers be involved—one for the lender and one for the borrower. The borrower will get unbiased advice, as mentioned earlier, ILA.

Do I have to visit a lawyer's office?

As part of the due diligence process, you must visit a lawyer's office. One of the most important reasons is the lawyer needs to verify your identity. The lawyer will ask you to bring two pieces of government-issued identification (e.g., a driver's license and a passport, not a health card). The lawyer also has to be satisfied that you are of sound mind, known legally as *capacity*, and that you are fully aware of the obligations and responsibilities associated with the loan.

The identification requirement reduces fraud and satisfies the lawyer's duty to comply with the obligation to "know his client."

CHAPTER 10

The Debt Miracle

• • •

The Debt Miracle is a phenomenon that occurs when you use low-rate private mortgage money to pay off high-rate debt. The private mortgage money pays off higher interest rates and higher minimum-payment debts with lower-interest-rate debt. The savings gained through lower monthly payments are then used to eliminate the original debt completely. The smart money uses lower rates to pay off higher ones.

Let's demonstrate this with a real-life example. Below is the before-and-after picture of the Debt Miracle in action. The borrower is a homeowner with unmanageable credit-card, line-of-credit, and automotive-loan debt.

Insider Secrets About How To Quickly and Easily Pay Off Your Debts

Before	Balance	Minimum Monthly Payment
First Mortgage	$455,000	$2,105
Auto Loan (it's a nice car!)	$30,000	$1,450
Credit Card 1	$7,800	$234
Credit Card 2	$15,000	$450
Credit Card 3	$11,000	$330
Line of Credit 1	$20,000	$600
Line of Credit 2	$30,000	$900
Total Non-Mortgage Debt	$113,800	
Total **Before** Payments		$6,069
Transaction Costs:		
Appraisal	$500	
Legal Lender	$1,200	
Independent Legal Advice	$800	
Broker fee	$5,500	
Lender fee	$5,500	
Total Funds Required	$127,300	
After		
First Mortgage	$455,000	$2,105
Second Mortgage	$127,300	$1,444
Total **After** Payments		$3,549
Monthly Savings	$2,520	

In just over three years of using a disciplined approach, the borrower was able to use the savings of $2,520 per month and eliminate the entire debt. Even if the homeowner only applied half of the monthly savings to the debt, it would be eliminated in just over five and a half years.

Compare the Debt Miracle approach to the minimum payment on most credit cards. Following the minimum-payment schedule, you will be paying that card off for decades, which is exactly what the banks want!

www.ingramcontent.com/pod-product-compliance
Lightning Source LLC
Chambersburg PA
CBHW070108210526
45170CB00013B/786